James & Nora

Portrait of Joyce's Marriage

Since her debut novel *The Country Girls*, Edna O'Brien has written over twenty works of fiction along with biographies of *James Joyce* and *Lord Byron*. She is the recipient of many awards including the Irish PEN Lifetime Achievement Award, the American National Art's Gold Medal, the Ulysses Medal and the PEN/Nabokov Award. She also received the David Cohen Lifetime Achievement Award in 2019. Born and raised in the west of Ireland, she has lived in London for many years.

James & Nora

Portrait of Joyce's Marriage

Edna O'Brien

WEIDENFELD & NICOLSON

First published in the United States in 1981 by
Lord John Press

This paperback edition published in 2020 by
Weidenfeld & Nicolson
an imprint of The Orion Publishing Group Ltd
Carmelite House, 50 Victoria Embankment
London EC4Y 0DZ

An Hachette UK Company

1 3 5 7 9 10 8 6 4 2

A CIP catalogue record for this book is
available from the British Library.

ISBN (Mass Market Paperback) 978 1 4746 1681 2
ISBN (eBook) 978 1 4746 1682 9

Printed in Great Britain by Clays Ltd, Elcograf S.p.A.

www.orionbooks.co.uk
www.weidenfeldandnicolson.co.uk

For Lee Brackstone,
Editor and friend

Foreword

I was a pharmaceutical student in Dublin in the 1950s but I craved to be a writer. I did not know how I would achieve this and I can safely say that my ambition outdistanced my talent. Then one day I bought for fourpence a second-hand book entitled *Introducing James Joyce* by T.S. Eliot and, reading the passages from *Portrait of an Artist,* I saw that Literature was not mysterious lofty stuff but the rough and tumble of everyday life. The description of the Christmas dinner destroyed by a political argument reminded me of my own experience and the uncurable conflicts within the lives of the people I knew at home. Since then hardly a day passes but I read something of Joyce's and of course my affections have changed with the years, as I am sure Joyce would wish them to. The lyric tenderness of those early stories still moves me, but the brilliance of *Ulysses* confounds and exalts me, and when I read the Anna Livia section of *Finnegans Wake* I feel that Joyce, with his 'lightning-lit reveries' is speaking to us from beyond the grave.

— Edna O'Brien
London, 1981

Would one but to do apart a lilybit her virginelles and, so, to breath, so, therebetween, behold . . .

————

His pale Galilean eyes were upon her mesial groove . . . O, the thunder of those loins!

————

If the shrew is worsted yet there remains to her woman's invisible weapon.

————

Love me, love my umbrella . . .

— James Joyce

1. FUNNOMINAL - PHENOMENAL.

2. DESPOND - DEJECTED OR LOSE CONFIDENCE.

3. IMPECUNITY - VERY LITTLE MONEY, UNABLE TO PAY; POVERTY.

4. JEjUNE - NAIVE, SIMPLISTIC + SUPERFICIAL.

5. SPURNING - REJECT WITH DISDAIN OR CONTEMPT

6. TERRENE - LIKE EARTH, EARTHLY

7. LECHER (OUS) - HAVING OR SHOWING EXCESSIVE OR OFFENSIVE SEXUAL DESIRE, LUSTFUL, LICENTIOUS.

8. BARD - CELTIC, PROFFESIONAL STORY TELLER OR VERSE MAKER.

9. PEERLESS - UNRIVALLED, UNEQUALLED = OR = TO BE W/OUT PEERS.

10. MUMMER - AN ACTOR IN A TRAD MASKED MIME'S PLAY

12. TIMONEER - //NAUTICAL// SOMEONE WHO STEERS A SHIP.

14. TITOVATION - SPRUCING UP,

J AMES JOYCE, poor Joist – 'a funnominal[1] man, supporting a gay house in
a slum of despond[2]'. He moved houses
– those haunted inkpots – scores of times.
His father before him had often moved house
and for an identical reason – impecunity[3]. His
name derived from the Latin and meant joy
but at times he thought himself joyless, that
Jejune[4] Jesuit spurning[5] Christ's terrene[6] body, a
lecher[7], a Christian brother in luxuriousness, a
bullock-befriending bard[8], a peerless[9] mummer[10],
a priestified kinchite[11], a quill-frocked friar, a
timoneer[12], a poolbeg flasher and a man with a
gift of Irish majacule[13] script. He shared with
Robert Burton a fascination and a curiosity

1

about women's apparel, but whereas to the author of *Anatomy of Melancholy* they were a source of wickedness, to James Joyce they were a source of spermic titivation [14] – three-quarter-length skirts cut on the bias, bloomers, stockings of purest silk, a wad of cotton wool soaked in perfume were all 'but a spring to catch woodcocks'.

Mr Joyce was not immune to the faults of women, but he was a man who believed in the overcoming of obstacles by the use of one's wits. The marriage of Socrates and Xanthippe he commended because it helped Socrates to perfect the art of dialectic by having to contend daily with a shrew. Like many a young man he skirted the snares of love but, true to life, he fell unto tippition. 'O Charis! O Charissima! A more intriguant bambolina could one not colour up out of Bocccucia's Enameron. . . the myth inmid the air. Mother of moth!' To have an inkling of anyone else's ascension-descension into love is nearly impossible, but to understand James Joyce's is dazzling, daunting, metamorphosing and imponderable. Here there is no truck with pots and pans, no normality. There is at once a reality weird in its searchingness, and a transformation wherein women are put on pedestals for litanies – 'Opals and pearls, warm lights, broken music'. The molecules of the body shuttling to and fro, as the artist in the man weaves and unweaves woman's image and the man in the artist desecrates and considers the stains on her drawers. Forever mingling the genitalia and the transubstantial. He carried a miniature pair of women's drawers in his pocket but unaccountably lost them one day just as Leopold Bloom might have done. Women are like rivers that flow in their own ineluctable way. Chatter chatter, teaseforhim, toesforhim, tossforhim. Exultance. Idiosyncrasy, Consummation. A ravelled mind giving values, dimensions and properties that do not exist except in the dreamer's desire for the impossible. Practical though he was in his delineation of the human anatomy, and in his description of the air, the streets and the shop fronts of his native Dublin, it is nevertheless impossible to decide what was real and what was figment. Admitting to being phenomenally egotistical and unused to compromise, nevertheless he fell in love. We know that he and the future Mrs Joyce eloped from Ireland, lived permanently in rented rooms, were hounded by debt, and that Mrs Joyce did not read much and did not care to cook. She bore the same name as the barnacle goose which he took to be an augury. He liked wild geese, gannets and migratories. The auguries that birds brought were suckerassousyoceanal. Their actual marriage did not take place until twenty-three years later and then it was a tame, twilight event in a registry office;

embarked upon for practical reasons so that their children could inherit his estate. But love, as Joyce would say, does not gallop on the rice-course of matrimony. For a long time they were fondly affianced.

> Pillowed on my coat she had her hair,
> earwigs in the heather scrub my hand
> under her nape, you'll toss me all. O
> wonder!

He could say that, he did say that, but did he not also say that Irish women were the cause of all moral suicide. He identified his mother with the Catholic Church, which he thought to be the scullery maid of Christendom. On both mothers he waged open and unrepentant war. His mother an umbiliacal drudge. Packing his secondhand clothes for him, as he prepares to set out for Paris, his mother tells him of her prayers, that away from home he may learn what the heart is and what it feels. Piety and sentiment he spat upon. It unnerved and disgusted his bantering soul. Just as his country did. He left it for fear he might succumb to the national disease, which was provincialness, wind-and-piss philosophising, crookedness, vacuity and a verbal spouting that reserved sentiment for God and for the dead. Despite the fact that he left his mother, he could not banish or repudiate her and he was to be haunted by her memory. Love is a paradox. Everything about Joyce was paradoxical. His grand schemes to buy things aligned to his humiliating debt. His pride in the sovereignity of fatherhood when he so desperately wanted to be woman. His clown-cum-hero Leopold Bloom felt himself to be father of all his race but is obsessed by the idea of birth and motherhood. Mr Bloom finds himself in the precincts of Hollis Street Maternity

Hospital where Mrs Mina Purefoy, 'the wan with the Methodist husband', has been accouched for three days and is lying with the vinegared hankerchief on her forehead, her belly writhing because the child's head is too big and is trying to butt its way out.

First he tickled her
Then he patted her
Then he passed the female catheter.
For he was a medical
Jolly old medi . . .

Womb dread, womb longing, womb envy. The doubled-up head inside the swollen woman puts the pleasurable spermic idealisations out of Bloom's mind. He still quaffs the porter with his cronies but he cannot forget the bully boy struggling to get out.

James Joyce was the first surviving son of two people for whom marriage was an escal-

ating disaster. His father had to say that the
name Murray – his wife's maiden name – stank
in his nostrils. The name Joyce stood for joy.
James Joyce's sympathies inclined towards his
father, whom he actually forgave for being Mr
Himmyshimmy, a blighty, a reeky, a lighty, a
scrapy, a babbly, a ninny, a dirty thief. But for
his mother tenderness was withheld. She may
have been too solicitous, asking him at six or
seven not to mix with rough boys at school.
Or she may have been too possessive. When a
young girl, Eileen Vance, wrote him a ditty –

Oh Jimmy Joyce you are my darling, you
are my looking glass night and morning.

– the mother intercepted the letter. He bore
her a grudge that persisted to her deathbed
and after – 'Her glazing eyes, staring out of
death, to shake and bend my soul. On me
alone . . . Her hoarse loud breath rattling in

horror . . . Her eyes on me to strike me down.'

From Paris he was soon recalled by the ubiquitous, never-failing, cryptic, heart-needling Irish telegram — 'Mother dying come home.' Needless to say, he had to borrow the fare to come back. On the boat journey, as he saw the cliffs of Dover, he mused not on the dying woman but on the boulevards from whence he had come, on the couples and the prostitutes with perfumed bodies, chattering lips and warm, humid smells. He saw too that the sea moved like the scales of music and that it was capable of making notes in his head. The mother did not die then but lived on, causing her exasperated, inebriated husband to stand at the foot of her bed and cry out, 'Die and be damned to you.' Her son would not promise to do his Easter duty so that the mother would die as she had lived in torment, her image would be transmitted to the sea — grey, sweet, mother, snot-green, scrotum-tightening. When she had gone she appeared to him in a dream, her body wasted within its loose brown grave clothes, giving off an odour of wax and rosewood, her breath mute and reproachful.

For the large and motherless family it was a case of flits by moonlight as they moved house again and again to avoid landlord and bailiff. They lived on credit loans and the sales of anything saleable. They referred to the bailiff as His Lordship. They would move furniture in a handcart at night to a new abode where the new rent collector would not trace them for a week and then they would move again in the moonlight. Joyce was always borrowing. He tried to raise a fund for himself by retrieving pawn tickets, he tried to borrow from his fellow medical students when they wrote down his witticisms. He was at once proud and incapable of humiliation. He made many mistakes, but he himself said that a man of genius makes no mistakes and that all his actions, however feckless, however cruel, are portals of discovery. He had to quit the medical school because of lack of funds, but as well there was perhaps a lack of conviction. For him and the large family of brothers and sisters it was a question of scutter and noserags and bread and dripping. He wore second-hand breeches which of course he credited with the possibility of having previously belonged to some poxy bowsy, which in turn would infect him. Drink, the Irish opium, was his solace. Only the sacred pint could unbind his tongue, and naturally an excess of sacred pints had him prostrated in his own mulberry-coloured multicoloured multitudinous vomit. The family diet was tea, fried bread and dripping, their arguments fired by hangover, their repartee quick, unaffectionate and bitter. At that time in Dublin prostitution was carried on as publicly as in Algiers. The clientele were sailors,

British Tommy army officers and privates who went in closed cabs at night. Last but not least were the medical students, the jolly old medicals, and Joyce the lapsed medical student among them. So limp with leching, they betook themselves to the pelvic basin of the icky licky micky red-light district in the Rings End Road where hung out Tresh Nellie, Rosalie and the Coalquay whore. No doubt the brothels did not have the mad or exotic grotesque fascination that Joyce later wrote about, but they were where he found his much-desired abasement. The establishment Joyce singled out to immortalise in *Ulysses* was run by Mrs Bella Cohen, whose main ambition in life was to send her son to Oxford.

I gave it to Nellie
To stick in her belly
The leg of the duck
The leg of the duck.

Whatever Joyce beheld, he treated himself and his readers to visions unparalleled – gaudy women with little gold stibble teeth, a lady in a mop cap and crinoline with leg-of-mutton sleeves, hair in a net and underneath her chemise a little brown scapular of the Lamb of God to keep her from sin. One woman is in scarlet bloomers and a jacket slashed with gold, the next in a one-piece gown of moonlight blue, some who are in slips, others who do it in the shake of a lamb's tail, those who might soil a love letter in an unspeakable manner, those with little soft palms who soon surrender and the hoity-toity who threaten to fillet a man, vivisect him, put stars and stripes on his breeches, dig their spurs into him and, as it would seem, administer punishment while he is liking it and licking it. Stephen Dedalus, who was the impersonation of Joyce, confronts his dead mother there in leper grey, and in answer to her beseeching he says, 'Shite' and smashes the chandelier with his ash plant.

O, Kinch, thou art in peril. Get thee a breechpad.

was his admonition to himself. Much as the lapsed Jesuit would revel over sinful, seedy Bella Cohen's establishment, the latent Jesuit would deem a journey to such a place as a jaunt to the gates of Hell while the ex-medical student would blame the temperature of the testicles. Yet not there in Rings End Road, permeated with fog, were the entrails of his being laid bare. He longed to copulate with a soul. What we long for, it seems we eventually get. Whish. A gull. Gulls. Far calls. Cries. And her very own namesake the barnacle goose, which must have been a wholesome augury to him who was augury-ridden. Clinging. Crustaceous. Nora Barnacle. Bright, chatty, he thought she sauntered into his life. He mistook her bafflement, perhaps, for self-possession. A country girl from Galway who worked as a chambermaid in a hotel. Joyce asked what might Caesar have lived to do had he believed both the soothsayer and his wife, Fulvia, had he not gone out on the Ides of March to be killed. It was ordained. The lawless lover in him was growing tired of scortatory love. Whores were bad conductors of emotion and he longed to copulate with a soul. His brother Stanislaus, who had a somewhat disgruntled view of the human race, thought that if James longed to copulate with a soul he ought to get himself born anywhere other than Ireland.

It was June. June the tenth. Barnacle day. He saw her in Nassau Street and they stopped to talk. She thought his blue eyes were those of a Norseman. He was twenty-two, she was twenty. They made a date and arranged to meet the following day at Number One Merrion Square, outside the house of Sir William Wilde. On that corner Joyce had the dubious advantage of being able to see in four different directions, of being able to catch sight of her either walking towards him or alighting from a tram. We all know the trepidation, the ingrained despairingness of these waits. His was no exception. She did not show up. He wrote to her that night and said that he had looked for a long time at a crop of reddish-brown hair and had to concede that it was not hers. Might they have another appointment. His tone was light but no doubt his intention determined. In this jaunty, fairly illiterate girl, whose plumpness might have appealed to Rubens, Joyce was to seek and find the earth mother, dark, formless, made beautiful in moonlight. Joyce was a Dubliner, Nora was from Galway. She was to bring in her jingles, her stories, her pisreogs, the echoes of her ancestory, the other half of Ireland – soil, gloom, moon-grey nettles and muttering rain. Yeats had said that when he fell in love with Maud Gonne MacBride it was then all the troubling of his life began. For Joyce, at least at first, it was a case of physical and mental transport, and this young girl was a summons to his blood. As terribly as Abelard tried to crush and exorcise his own and Heloise's libidinousness, so did Joyce try to ignite theirs.

He tried to be her, to know her as in her convent days in Galway when the Sisters of Mercy prepared her for First Holy Communion, her scallywagging days when she and her friends made dates with a man in the church and then devoured the box of chocolates he had given them. Nothing was to be kept from him. He wanted to strip her of all mask and all clothing, to pass through her, into her secret, inviolate individuality. With what tenacity did he investigate and pursue it. The past of this girl obsessed him — her little trite girlhood

props, things such as garters, bracelets, cream
sweets and a pale green lily of the valley not
as a flower but as a brooch. He went in as a
deep-sea diver must go, to discover everything
about her. She was to be earth and formless,
she was to be dark occasionally made beautiful
by moonlight (rather like a glowworm), she
was only to be half conscious of her myriad
fluid-like instincts. The sum of her past in
Galway in the little things she did, like take
a bite at a snap apple, steal a cube of sugar,
or listen under doorways for a pre-natural
whisper that would tell her the initials of her
future husband, these were to be the first of
her revelations but by no means the last. Her
chastity he would confirm in her adultery.
And when he said such and such a thing
and she said, 'I know what's talking there,'
meaning his sex, he felt a terrible pre-aged
melancholic reproach in her. Like womankind
she was older, wiser yet to their children he

was more mother than she. Nora was both child and mother, describing the outskirts of Galway, woods, fields, the cows, the cowslips, the covey of girls in the warm hills undressing, seeing their bodies as wild roses.

Once she acquired a snood to put over her auburn hair, to gird her wildness, another time she donned man's clothes, another time she stood on a dung hill chewing a head of raw cabbage so as to be treated secretly to the sound of the name of the man that was to be her husband. She was his precious darling, his pouting Nora, his little brown head. He loved her soft voice. In her company he left aside his jeering, contemptuous nature. She was invited to a concert-hall room to hear him sing. He warned that he would be nervous, but he did not realise his pianist would become so nervous as to quit and leave Joyce to hammer out the notes for himself and sing – 'Down by the Sally Gardens'.

For entertainment they walked. They could not afford to do anything else. Yet he was not blind to what he saw – the watch towers, the murmuring waters, the fishful stream and the empathy of the mighty dead. He was not to assign it to paper until long after, but he saw and noted it all. He saw the space of the sky, the ever-changing evening violet, the dark, dripping gardens with their ash pits, the soggy flower beds, the stables where a coachman combed the horses and of course the sea, the seaweed, the warm sand, the wavelets, the sharp shingle, the water mirroring the high drifting clouds. Next day she wrote to say that in his company she always felt herself to *be*, her spirit took leave of her body in sleep, and the loneliness which she felt in his absence faded away in his presence. Joyce, who saw and scrutinized every word, recognised at once that these were not the words of a girl who invoked charms and made beds and emptied chamber pots for a living. He guessed rightly. She had copied the letter from a book of etiquette at the time. Possibly he loved her even more for it. The waters were getting fathoms deep and in them the minnows whose movement he likened to that inside his trouser's fly – God becomes man becomes fish becomes barnacle goose becomes feather bed mountain.

As he saw more of her he felt obliged to tell her how he had hated and disavowed mother church, how he had loved and espoused the brandle buttocking of the ladies in Nighttown. She did not want to know. She must. She would have to know how remote he was and how flawed. She would have to know that he entered the social order of Ireland as a deliberate vagabond. There was Stephen the acolyte and Bloom the lecher and they alternated. One day it was her knickers and the next day it was his soul on the brink of hers and by night it was himself making half-hearted plans to flee by going with an actors' company. But he was already bound. The proverb that Leromontov tells in *A Turkish Tale* applied to Joyce too – 'Whereupon is written upon a man's forehead at birth he is not fated to forego.' Maybe it was those dog's eyes of hers. Like Anne Hathaway. She hath a way. By cock she was to blame. She had put come hither on him. He would sleep with her glove beside him and had to remark that it behaved itself very properly, like its owner. He would buy her a gift of gloves but where would he get the money. He was scrounging in the name of the crucified Christ and getting volleys of refusal. No rhymed with woe. Old cronies asked for the previous loans to be returned but Joyce parried, 'Molecules all change. I am other I now. Other was the borrower'! Still he bought her the gloves. Perhaps he used the payment for a story, 'The Sisters', which appeared in

The Irish Homestead, which he called The Pigs' Monthly.

His letters written to her in the morning would, miraculously, be delivered before lunch and he would have a reply before nightfall. She would run from her duties to the bedroom or the WC and read them. She learnt that she was to leave her stays at home because they were like a dragoon's, that she was to come without skirts in order to receive his papal benediction, that the power of indulgence had been vested in him by Pope Pius X and that she must know that it was from such muddy pools that angels call forth a spirit of beauty. Her kisses were like the singing of canaries. He was her brother in luxuriousness, her Christian brother and agonising Jew. To him she was simple-minded, excitable, impotent, sleepy and she broke all before her. But she was no casual comrade in lust: 'fire fulplay, frisking in the kool kurkle dusk of lushness'.

23

He was drinking her mountain dew. He could not say that he loved her, he would not say it. She pressed. He would not say it. He could say that he was very fond of her, that he desired to possess her wholly, that he admired and honoured her and that he sought to secure her happiness. Love it may not be, but need it was. She became the breast between him and God and death – 'How I hate God and death, how I like Nora.' She was still sniffing around for the word love. She could not have plumbed both the ruthlessness and the meticulousness of his thinking, and she could not have known that for him, as for any great writer, to say love is merely conditional since his soul insists on the state of emotional flux and actuality depends forever on the partial denial of what is, or has been, in order to give new life to it. He doubted and questioned who he was and what he was – 'that which I was is that which I am and that which in possibility I may come to be.

24

So in the future, the sister of the past, I may see myself as I sit here now but by reflection from that which then I shall be.'

He applied for a teaching post in Zurich in a Berlitz School and was accepted. It was then his touching began in earnest and he asked a friend, Starkey, to get from his father's shop one toothbrush, and powder, a nail brush, a pair of boots, a coat and a vest. He must have relied on Nora Barnacle to have her own toothbrush and tooth powder. She was expecting a little legacy from a grandmother in Galway, but all expectation of money turned out to be futile either for Joyce or for his girl. When they set out from the docks on their clandestine adventure it was shrouded in secrecy and possibly dread. When they arrived in Zurich there was no vacancy, and so they went to Trieste where there was none either, and finally they settled in the naval town of Pola. Soon a letter to Stanislaus tells how Nora is lonely whenever he is away, and how her boot pinches. Were her family by any chance putting advertisements in the paper to ask of her whereabouts, did the girls who had worked with her in the hotel think her 'snotty'? He earned two pounds a week by teaching English, mostly to officers of the Austrian Navy. He looked forward to the day when he could get a new suit and have his teeth fixed. They rose at nine and partook of chocolate. They lunched in a locanda opposite, surprisingly had dinner there also, and then on to a cafe for Joyce to read the French newspapers. Very soon Nora became pregnant. They quarrelled, but then they would make up. She curled his hair with her tongs, and when for an instant she withdrew her loving looks he was beside himself and would tremble. A rift happened in a restaurant once and he wrote a beseeching letter to know what had come between them.

Yet there was one strand of betrayal in him: not only did he think he might leave her — ('There is an anxiety at the back of my mind for which I want to be ready materially,') — but told his brother Stanislaus some of her woman's secrets, her early love affairs, confiding a near-seduction by a curate with black curly hair, and a thrashing which she got from her uncle during which he went down on his knees in a kind of orgasmic convulsive fit. Stanislaus did not like her and withheld respect for her. Yet Joyce told him these juicy things and added, 'Pretty little story, eh?' And what did Nora think? She said to tell Stan, 'She was axing at him.' She put Xs for kisses and, like Molly Bloom, chose to turn a blind eye to her brother-in-law's disapproval of her. Writing was something that did not interest her and she even questioned the validity of her husband using up reams of paper to write what he was then calling his epiphanies. She often sang when dressing, she sang:

Old Tom Gregory

Has a big menagerie . . .

She licked the jam off its sealing-paper cover and regaled him with droll country wit. But there was a less sunny side to her. There was the helpless exile who lay in a dark room and cried. She was reluctant to go out into the street without him, for fear of being insulted. She spoke thirty words of Triestine dialect, could not learn French and disliked Italian cooking, thinking it too sloppy. The director of the Berlitz School said, upon meeting her, that she was not worthy of Joyce. To this Joyce said that a man would need a degree of self-stultification to fathom that one. Anyhow he decided that only would-be thinkers or feminists would expect a woman to be a man's equal. For all his ribaltry about it, it was plain that there were problems. The heat made her breathless and powerless, the cold gave her

chilblains. She often said that she longed to
hear and see a kettle boiling on a hob. She
moped. He feared that she was sapping his
natural gaiety. So here we have this young
girl, in a short brown dress, with thick coils
of hair, living with a man whose body she
could entice but whose mind she could not
comprehend. He saw that she was one of those
plants that could not be safely transplanted.
She cried a lot. He feared for the moroseness
of the child that she would bring forth and
felt pity as he watched her fail to make the
baby clothes that she was trying desperately
to copy from a pattern. She was weakening his
natural cheerfulness and, hearing mistakenly
that Ibsen had left his wife, the same thought
occurred to him. They spent nights of horrible
melancholy, one of which she salvaged for him
by quoting a line of his poetry – 'O sweetheart
hear you your lover's tale'. She had misquoted
it, but her very utterance had miraculously

revived his flagging belief in himself as a poet. Also their estrangements were a spur to their lusts.

They had reckoned that their first child was due in August, but not unsurprisingly they had miscalculated the event. Joyce was about to go bathing when Nora was struck down with a pain that seemed remarkably like indigestion. Their landlady summoned the midwife. Six hours later, when he heard that he had a son and heir, he took it in his arms, hummed operatic airs to it and predicted that it would have the singing voice of its father and its grandfather. This was a hope that he never forsook.

When the telegram 'Son born Jim' reached Dublin, Mr Joyce senior first wept, then set about borrowing the money to send a telegram of congratulation. Earlier on Joyce had been referring to it in letters to his brother as the 'interesting event', but now that a son was born, amazement, emotion and unwonted sentiment were unleashed. He said the most important thing that can happen to a man is the birth of a child. The runaway James was forgiven. Mr Joyce senior said the news gave him a 'Christmas morning feeling.' Stanislaus predicted that the birth would enhance his brother's status in Dublin and how his friendly enemies would be overwhelmed. It was as if Joyce was the first man to father a child, so widespread were the congratulations. Stanislaus confessed that his own affections were ignoble and sluggish compared with Jim's. He predicted a great relationship building up between father and son.

Years after, James Joyce believed that a mysterious malady had caught hold of his children when they were very young. In fact he believed that he and his common-law wife had not loved them enough. In a sense they were still massively in a state of love with each other. Joyce was only twenty-five and caught up in the double exhaustion of teaching and writing. His wife and he were still physically besotted. But poor. They moved to Rome, where Joyce had taken a position in a bank, a task to which he was constitutionally alien and unsuited. 'Bethelemites' was how he termed them. There was not a day that they were not in search of a room, in search of an inn, in search of a meal, in search of a pupil. He was fond of his son, he said, but his own spiritual barque was on the rocks. He would rage and call on anything to change 'his curse O God state of affairs'. He would stay too long in the tavern and come home to a disgruntled wife, flapping like a rag in a breeze. He said he would not be surprised if she didn't unload a second male child for the dynasty. Genius and parenthood make bad bedfellows. Dante may have been his spiritual food, but Rome was nauseous. He associated it with death, corpses and assassination. After all, the one most important feature of Rome was the foundation of the Roman Church. He likened her to a hussy who offers herself among perfumes, flowers, hymns and sacred music but is stinking on her outdated throne. He noted that the subtle Romans broke a lot of wind and that Shelley's granddaughter was left-handed. Tired he may have been, but nevertheless he went to the library to look up the Vatican Council's Declaration of the Pope's infallibility so that he could see it for himself. His mind was on his native city, recalling streets, laundries, a certain kind of lamp, street women, dirty sheets, Poolbeg Street, and the Dublin water supply.

When they looked for lodgings they would be turned away because of having a small child. Nora would wait first in a cafe and then in a cinema while he arrived late at night with the money just received for the private lesson. They would have dinner and then search for a room where the tariff suited their pitiable means. They slept head to toe to avoid the risk of future Joyces. The next morning he would go to the bank, Nora and Georgio would vacate the room at noon, go to the cinema and re-wait in a cafe for him to arrive with the money from the private lesson so that they could do the exact same thing. If only she had kept a diary. Of what was she thinking? Her loneliness? Galway? Her family? Their future? She even delivered a complaining letter to him at his bank, but all he could do was blow his nose in it. As a man with the Pentecostal tongues of fire he could conjure up imaginary worlds, but for her there were no such ascensions and there was no money, no girlfriends, no chatter and no clothes. He later expressed a memory of love's history as being stars that burned with a pure though distant intensity. He was close to mental exhaustion. Any ideas he had had about socialism were quashed, so here he was working in a bank, giving private tuition, and also setting down for eternity incalculable and effulgent images. No pen, no ink, no table, no room and no quiet. They had pasta for Christmas dinner, but he was pleased to be able to say that he had bought his little son a rocking horse. He loved giving gifts and in *Finnegans Wake* he enables Anna Livia to give prodigious gifts to her thousand and one children. His brother Stanislaus received the full surge of these impecunious cries. He would be told to send ten crowns and enclose it in good thick paper so that Joyce's employer in the bank would not see it. He would be told to be on the alert to send twenty or thirty more in a week and to give full credence to the fact that Giorgio now needed a new sheet, and that Giorgio broke windows and drinking vessels freely. Joyce complained that his teeth were rotting and so was his soul. Life, as he said, was slipping from him like water from a muslin bag. If Stanislaus had not the money, he was to try this one or that one, another teacher, another pupil, another merchant, anyone. The money was to be wired. 'Buck up,' Stanislaus was told. If there is any relationship in which Joyce's qualities as a monster are brought to full fruition it is towards his brother. – 'Enchainted, dear sweet Stainusless'.

His dislike of Rome caused him to hand in his resignation in a burst of pique. He toyed with the idea of going to Marseilles, except that he did not have the money for the postage stamp to apply for a position there. Despite sleeping head to foot, Nora had again conceived. So it was back to Trieste. He taught, he wrote articles and soon he fell ill with rheumatic fever. This he believed he contracted from his many tumbles in the gutter. First we feel, then we fall. While he was in one wing of the hospital his daughter was born in the paupers' ward and he insisted that she be named Lucia after the Patron Saint of eyes. When Nora was discharged from the hospital she was given twenty crowns in charity. She came home to a small flat, a noisy son, an over-worked brother-in-law and her own depleted self. It is hard for love to keep alive under such conditions. He thought of rash schemes to make money – 'A Joyce of all trades'. Four business men were roped in to finance it. They would open a cinema in Dublin. It was when he returned there that his love for Nora was rekindled and reinvoked with the same passion, the same rapture as at first. A flood of letters crossed the Irish Sea as the sacred and profane flame of love was re-ignited. It is amazing that the hierarchy did not divine them and seize the mailbags. They are frank, rabid and founded on lust. The two parts of her body which did dirty things were the loveliest to him, her arse being his favourite. He wished for her spluttering lips, for her heavenly exciting filthy words, for the smell of her dirty fat girlish farts; he would do as she said and lie down with the letter and pull at himself hoping she was tickling her little cockey and at the same time writing to him.

He found a vacant premises in Mary Street, had it wired, fitted with seats and even chose three films, which he believed would generate tender sentiments. His own sentiments had run amok. Nora alternated between whore and queen. She was a dark blue mountain flower, while also being a strumpet whose hot solicitations would spur him on. A torrent of spermic odes were dispatched across the Irish Sea.

He was envisaging her as she summoned him into a room to reprimand him, and there, seated on a chair, her fat thighs apart, her face a deep red with anger, a cane in her hand was the chastising woman. She was to flog flog flog. He would be ever grateful if she fucked him dressed in full outdoor costume with hat and veil, her boots muddy as she straddled him. Then again with the frilly drawers, again with the crimson flower in her behind, and these couplings were to be enacted in every quarter of their apartment including the dark well of the stairs and the darker closet.

His children were five or six at the time and he was unaware, though later to witness his daughter's jealousy and rivalry towards her mother. So from his native city, the matrix of all his creative works, these letters were dispatched. Like all great lecherous promisings it began to taper somewhat as he neared home and there were instead vignettes of his lolling on a chair, watching her prepare the meals and talking talking talking talking.

For her part she seems to have complied perfectly with his voracious fantasies, and in his father's bickering house in Fontenoy Street he would receive her hot letters in which she described her masturbations, her hand hard at work through the slit of her drawers. His two sisters Eva and Eileen, who were preparing to come to Trieste, would hardly have embarked on the journey if they knew that their future home was a den of lawless lust.

As he got nearer to returning he was becoming the knight of the rueful coun-tenance, and she reassumed for him the role of the little mother who would take him into the dark sanctuary of her womb, would be a shelter and a refuge. I wonder if there is some madness in me, or is love madness, he had had to ask himself. Perhaps, yes. Love for him was not unlike the images that would crowd his narratives, the shuttling to and fro of startling and contradictory feelings. She fed his uncertainty. She even said in a letter – in direct contrast to one of her hot scatterbrain little notes – that she might leave him, and while giving her the full benefit of verbal understanding, even permitting her to forget her children, he then stoutly professed that he could not live, that he could not go on living, that he was simply staring at the words she had written, desolated. They were masters at vacillation. Later they read and liked the works of Sacher-Masoch.

Never far from the throes of love are the fangs of jealousy. In his native city the need for his compatriots to hurt him was twofold. He had been sending chapters of his novel *Stephen D.* to his friends, and he must have known how they would also see themselves scurrilosed and how they would see that they had let a genius slip through their fingers. Cosgrave, the other contender for Nora's hand, said it was unfair of Joyce to frig the one idea about love which Cosgrave had given him via Nora. Vincent the Rum Rooster himself. On the alternate nights when Joyce did not see Nora she had seen Cosgrave. They had met outside the museum, they had walked down

the canal to the banks of the Dodder, there she
had held Cosgrave's hand, kissed him and what
else? Joyce had got it from the culprit's lips.
Was all over between them? Was their love
broken? Was Giorgio their son? Were not the
blood stains for her deflowering very scant?
Was she lying down in the fields near by the
Dodder when she kissed the other? Did she
place her hand on the other's person and talk
softly as she did with him? He appeals to her
almost as if she could incite his pain. He asks if
there is any hope for him. He even thinks that
he might have consumption, so terrible is his
grief. Naturally, to have learned of this betrayal
in Dublin was the most plausible place in the
world. Had they not thrown quicklime in the
eyes of his hero Parnell, and was he not in some
secret part of himself longing for betrayal? So
the letters of accusation flowed across the sea
for the few days while he believed that it was
true. He cried out that his faith in her was

broken. It is a pity that Nora was not a fluent letter writer, because we do not know what she thought or if she felt a secret triumph. Was she disappointed in a man who said, 'Is there any hope of my happiness,' or was she in fact glad of his dependence on her?

It was not long before he learned that it was a dirty trick that Cosgrave had played on him, and so he would try to make amends by sending her shell cocoa and an oath of love. The old fever was reawakened. He was hers. She held him in her hand like a pebble. From her he had learned the secrets of love. She must bear with him in all his wandering moods. His body would soon penetrate into hers and O that his soul could too and O that he could nestle in her womb, be fed by her blood, sleep in the warm secret gloom of her body. He procured for her a necklace which he himself had designed and which he revelled in describing. It was in a flat square case lined with orange silk. There were five little dice of ivory strung together on a gold fetter and on tablets of ivory there was an engraving – 'Love is unhappy when love is away'. He believed that ornaments had a magical virtue, were a talisman against the evil forces of the world. Two very distinct images of her haunted him – one she had come to him in her chemise as he lay asleep, the second her look of helplessness at the railway station, unable to say goodbye. They would fight the cowardly plot. He was, as he said, absurdly jealous of her past and he dreaded going back to her native Galway lest he might be shown a picture of her as a girl and then start to think of her sauntering to Mass and giving some other boy one of her long glances. He visualised her in a hundred poses – shameful, virginal, langourous.

He went to Galway and heard from her mother a song that she had loved – 'The Lass of Aughrim'. He pretended to be buying a house in a certain street in order to have a peep into a room where Nora had once slept. His jealousy waned somewhat as her mother recalled her girlish exploits, her rhymes, her songs, and above all, her winsome ways. But the jealousy had lodged and would be put to great literary purpose. 'In the very core of my ignoble heart I longed to be betrayed by you,' says the character in *Exiles* who wants his wife to become his friend's lover. The wife in turn thinks that the two men will only be united by both of them having the knowledge of her body. Carnal knowledge, while being a betrayal, would also be a uniting. They were partners now in crime. She had killed the virginity of her soul. She was sinner as previously she had not been. As it got nearer to his return home a shyness overcame him and he asked if he could loll in a chair. Her hair was to be in good colour, with no cinders, she was to show the appear-

ance of money and could she get some black
underclothes.

It was their only big rift. The separateness
that came later would be the universal one,
a separateness of the mind. He was about to
embark on *Ulysses*, a book that would take
seven years of unbroken labour, twenty
thousand hours of work, havoc to body and
brain, nerves, perspiration and unreasonable
agitation at the slightest sound. He who had
vowed to forge the conscience of his race was
now poised to defy tradition and do a Humpty
Dumpty on the English language. By the time
he had reached the end he was indeed another
man and had a staggering number of eye com-
plaints – glaucoma, iritis, cataract, nebula in
the pupil, conjunctivitis, dissolution of the
retina, blood accumulation, abscesses and
one-tenth normal vision. His husbandry going
into his work and nights lost in drink. He
quaffed the nectar cup. Absinthe proved to be

too strong and now it was white wine which
he said was like electricity of a highest piss
of the highest archduchess. Red wine was a
beefsteak. Nora would scold, sulk, sometimes
leave and go to another hotel. Deputations
came to bring her back. She would wish aloud
that she had never met anyone by the name of
James Joyce, yet back she came. Indignation,
compromise and muddle. All our lives. Again
and again he insisted that cheerfulness took
hold of him when he sat down to drink and
when he sat down to write. If there was to
be a sign printed on his person it was to be
'Beware of the Miserers'. But he was changing.
He said himself that we have not lived until
we have conceived of life as a tragedy. He was
coming to see people more as archetypes than
as real people. Nora Barnacle was to undergo
mutation. She would be the primal source for
Molly Bloom although she herself said, with
her customary drollness, that Molly Bloom

was much fatter. And what is Molly Bloom?
She is a marvel of licentiousness, noddle and
non-guilt. 'I unbuttoned him and took his out
and drew back the skin it had a kind of eye in
it they're all Buttons men'. Molly is as wise to
Bloom as to every creature walking on earth.
She had dispensed with maids, for what use
were they, stealing her potatoes and oysters,
cajoling Bloom and singing in the WC. She is
even thinking of procuring a young boy and
derives pleasure from imagining him seeing
her garters, the new ones making him turn
red, seducing him and knowing what boys
feel 'with that down on their cheek doing
that frigging drawing out the thing by the
hour'. She at once scolds and boasts of her
husband's plabbery, glaumming, ardour and
the black closed breeches he made her buy.
She remembers her labour when bringing
forth her daughter Millie and her happiness
on a hearthrug in Lombard Street when her

lover Blazes Boylan gave her mulled rum and a good time. Men and their yogeybogeybox. Women and their wiles. She can taste fancy cakes such as she saw in the shop and a corset she would like to get and the mountains and the meadows and the abundance of nature with fine cattle going about fields of oats, flowers, all sorts of shapes springing up out of the ditches, primroses and violets, her first kiss under a moorish wall, but above all she remembers the celebration of her own body, and the sure knowledge of her prowess with the opposite sex and her own unconditional surrender, which is inextricably bound up with the image of the crushed flower and the image of nature and of sea giving forth all that it has.

Writers are a scourge to those they cohabit with. They are present and at the same time they are absent. They are present by the fact of their continuing curiosity, their observing, their cataloguing minds, their longing to see into another person. But the longing is discharged into the work. The photographs of Nora with her growing children show us a solemn woman with an unreadiness to smile. She loved clothes and he indulged her in this, but clothes are a poor substitute for the first flush of undivided attention. The most of his time was spent in a semi-dark room with a rhyming dictionary, maps, street directories of Dublin, different coloured pencils, lost to the outside world.

Just as the imagination has to be rescued from abstraction, so too has the yearn for a new and romantic love. For all his scathingness and despite his unremitting intellect, Mr Joyce was a romantic when it came to women. Bed her, red her and tread her. He desired the female's stimulation. His first incursion into the clandestine realm was an attachment formed towards one of his pupils. A young girl with eyes like an antelope and twittering happy sing-song voice. Her name was Amalia Popper and she was the daughter of a Jewish merchant named Leopoldo. Joyce believed that he himself was Jewish in the bowels. He would arrive for the lesson wearing his father's old yellow waistcoat. The lesson itself was anything but convention. It was Joyce lolling on two chairs puffing away and making puns.

Mephistopholes = Mavis Toffeeless
Xmas cake = Chrissomis wake
De Profundis = Deepbrow fundigs

Amalia was made the heroine of a story, cooped up in a stone castle with coats of mail, guttering flames and gibbets. Yet he sensed that her false smile concealed a rancid yellow humour within the pulp of her eyes. She was too bourgeois. In the mirror of himself, that he saw in her, he beheld his decaying self.

She was the opposite to his Galway girl. A Semite in heavy, odourous furs. She gave his daughter a flower. He writes about it in his diary – blue flower, blue-veined child. Did Nora suspect? He rebuked himself – 'Easy now Jamesy. Did you never walk the streets of Dublin at night sobbing another name.' He delineates Amalia raising her arms to hoop her gown, his helping her, touching the web-soft edges, then peeping underneath at her little body in an orange shift. Like a fish she has silver scales. Cold, calm but besotted, he begs mister God for a touch.

Amalia loved her father and thus provided Joyce with a thread of jealousy which was necessary to prolong his obsession. She persecuted his mind. As it wore on, this attraction filled him with the foreknowledge of age, winter, dying, death and wastage of soul. The seed he had spent on her merely linguistic, elegiac. The piano in her apartment came to resemble a coffin. She greeted him wintrily. Stars were waning in the heavens. In short, he saw time's treacheries.

He was thirty-five when he next underwent the 'kinchite quiver'. It was not without its comic overtones. He observed a handsome young woman with a limp going down a street in Zurich. He followed to catch sight of her face and when he did his own face lit up, fused with the prospect of a love that was sudden but arbitrary. These impulses do not draw into question the validity of such attraction but merely warn us of its fleetingness on the choppy seas of reality. He watched for her each evening, followed her to her flat and was soon pursuing her with notes announcing his new-born passion. She was a pretty little animal, in a big hat with waving feathers. There was something frank and shameless about her despite the gentleness of her eyes. He himself was of the same age as Dante when he entered

'The night of his being'. Or Shakespeare when he met the dark lady of the sonnets. Martha Fleischmann. A pagan Mary. Rather precipitously, he complained of his own unhappiness without even considering hers. Two great egotists were at a temporary meeting point. She was a semi-aristocrat kept by a man and she spent her days preening herself, smoking and reading – a more languid Molly Bloom – romantic novels. He stood outside her window watching her read the letters from him, the letters that said, 'I had a fever waiting for you, I am a poor seeker in this world, perhaps I have lived too long, do you think of me, I see you coming towards me in black, young strange and gentle.' Reams of repressed sex and dizzying self-absorption. Her letters went to a secret address. In case she felt too exhausted or too nervous to write, he would send the return envelope all ready. A word would suffice, a yes, a no. Was she suffering as he was? Was she out of her mind? Certainly *he* was, when he told her that he looked at the paper every morning fearing to read her name in the death announcements. His wife cannot have known because she thought of him as her own preserve, and years later flew indignant when he was photographed with a fashionable lady who claimed that her bedside book was *Ulysses*. At any rate he met Martha, and even managed on his birthday to engineer a celebration at the house of his friend Frank Budgen. For the occasion he borrowed a ceremonial Jewish candlestick from an antique dealer for what he named a 'black mass'. For Martha the evening was overwhelming and had an element of excess and intrigue.

Next thing, he rudely learns that she is in a sanitorium suffering from her nerves, which she believes have been exacerbated by him, and her lover-guardian is asking Mr Joyce for recompense. Mr Joyce, who was afraid of dogs, thunder and any sudden noises, whose eyesight had begun to fade, was hardly the man to set out with his seconds and a pair of pistols for a duel in some wood at dawn. The man is mightier than the pistol. He managed to slither out of it. He succeeded in calming the irate guardian by means of over-timidity, suave human diplomacy and bluff. He did not hear from the lady again until she recommended him an eye doctor in his old age. It seems to have been the last of his botched flings.

Highhearted youth comes not again.

Gravity memory and mockery are what proceed.

When the time came that it was advisable for him to marry, he shelved his distaste for that monstrous institution and permitted it so that his children could inherit his estate. The wedding was in a registry office in London, but by then he was more concerned about his eyesight than about marriage. Things had changed. His intense, obsessive, solicitous over-love had transferred itself to his children, particularly to his daughter, Lucia, who resented her mother, who shouted out loud that she herself was sex-starved, in short Joyce-starved. Nora was altered too — cut off from him, when he made those voyages into his work and when he sent himself to the very extremities of mind to compose a language that no one had ever heard of and no one had foreseen. He was writing *Finnegans Wake* by then. A work conceived in a darkened room by a man with a darkened brain. The bat hour, the twilight hour. In writing it he relinquished a literary kingdom guessing his followers must desert him. Women were dolls and now he was only interested in their clothing. Nora's desire had also paled, and she could say like Anna

Livia — 'win me, woo me, wed me, ah weary me!'. She complained of life, caring for her recalcitrant daughter and sitting up with artists till all hours, bored stiff. 'Men', she said, 'were only up in your tail.' He had given her the keys to his heart and married her till delth to uspart. But Acoolsha he was changing and thinking of a daughter wife who would swim in her mother's hindmoist. The young girl has not the mossiness of the mother but something perhaps more modern, because she corresponds to the motor carriage, is a whisk, brisk sly spry spink spank sprint of a thing. It was on Lucia that his love was showered. She was distraught, unsound in mind, often hysterical, often beyond reach. Reverting to his youthful innocence, Joyce thought that a fur coat might cure her. He believed that she was no madder than he. He not only loved and trusted her but he substituted his own logic for hers and made her thoughts and

sentences his own. Mr Edmund Wilson said of
Finnegans Wake that, in it, husband and wife
are no longer polarised and will waken from
their night's sleep with a new polarisation.
The father, Wilson says, is pulling towards
the children, and the wife is withdrawing as
she sees her husband as a guilty, lecherous
bumpkin. Mr Joyce and his wife are said to
have sexually – though not of course emo-
tionally – severed when she was thirty-nine.
Her third child, born prematurely, had died
and that must have cast a dark shadow. Their
daughter, Lucia, became Joyce's 'inspiritcrice'.
The mother seeing, resenting and having to
accept – 'you're changing, acoolsha, you're
changing from me, I can feel. Or is it me is? .
. . A way a lone a last a loved a long the'.

By the time he wrote that he had already
repudiated love and said that when he heard
the word love he felt like puking. His repu-
diation was a gigantic, bitter and perverse

leap, an utter departure, a revolt from the man who enquired, who luxuriated about the little brown stain on her drawers and named her the blue mountain flower. It has in it all the trademarks of the sons and daughters of the Roman Catholic Church. It is in stark and disappointing contrast to Montaigne's ruminations about love in old age, in which he expressed the view that it would 'restore him to vigilancy, sobriety, grace and care of his person, in which it would ensure his countenance against the wrinkled frowns of age, reduce him to serious and wise study whereby he might procure more love and purchase more estimation of it, above all it would purge his mind from despair of itself'.

No one can say that Mr Joyce did not experience love as a man, and perpetuate it as if he were man and woman. The last and perhaps the eeriest lines he ever wrote are those at the end of *Finnegans Wake* when

Anna resolves to slip away: 'O bitter ending! I'll slip away before they're up. They'll never see. Nor know. Nor miss me. And it's old and old it's sad and old it's sad and weary I go back to you, my cold father, my cold mad father, my cold mad feary father'. Back to the father who wishes to be synonymous with the matrix. No man has ever wanted so, to be a woman. No man has composed and decanted words that so utterly depict the true and desperate heart of a true and desperate woman.

The Joyces moved to Switzerland soon after the outbreak of the Second World War. In January 1941 he was taken ill, his body writhing like a fish as he was brought to hospital. Upon operating it was found that he had had a duodenal ulcer for several years. He asked that his wife's bed be put next to his, but the request was refused. Mother and son were sent home and that night Joyce died. Nora survived him by a long number of years, but when she died there was no room on the hill next to him in the Fluntern. The blunder that attended their elopement, the births of their children and all their wanderings had not forsaken them in death. Noewhemoe! Finiche! Only a fadograph of a yestern scene.